OPTICAL ILLUSIONS
Coloring Book

KOICHI SATO

Dover Publications, Inc.
New York

Publisher's Note

This coloring book of optical illusions presents 30 brain-bending geometric designs by graphic artist Koichi Sato. Preying upon conventional notions of space and perspective, these patterns create dazzling visual paradoxes when examined.

These images present unlimited coloring possibilities. You may wish to carefully contrast the colors of different areas to maximize the optical effects of the patterns. However you choose to color them, these designs are sure to create striking and puzzling effects.

Copyright

Copyright © 1994 by Koichi Sato.
All rights reserved.

Bibliographical Note

Optical Illusions Coloring Book is a new work, first published by Dover Publications, Inc., in 1994.

International Standard Book Number

ISBN-13: 978-0-486-28330-2
ISBN-10: 0-486-28330-5

Manufactured in the United States by Courier Corporation
28330512
www.doverpublications.com

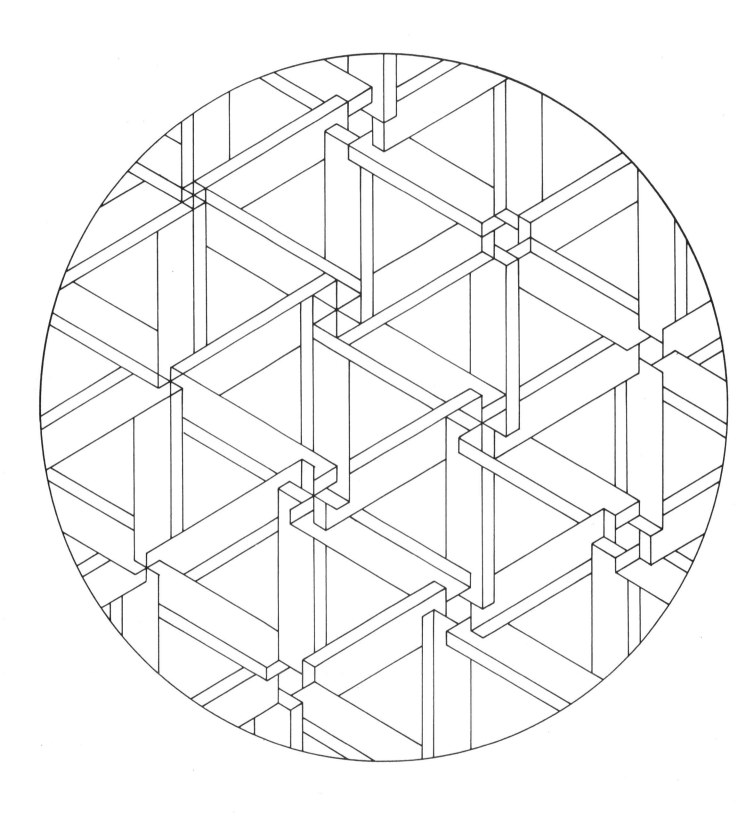

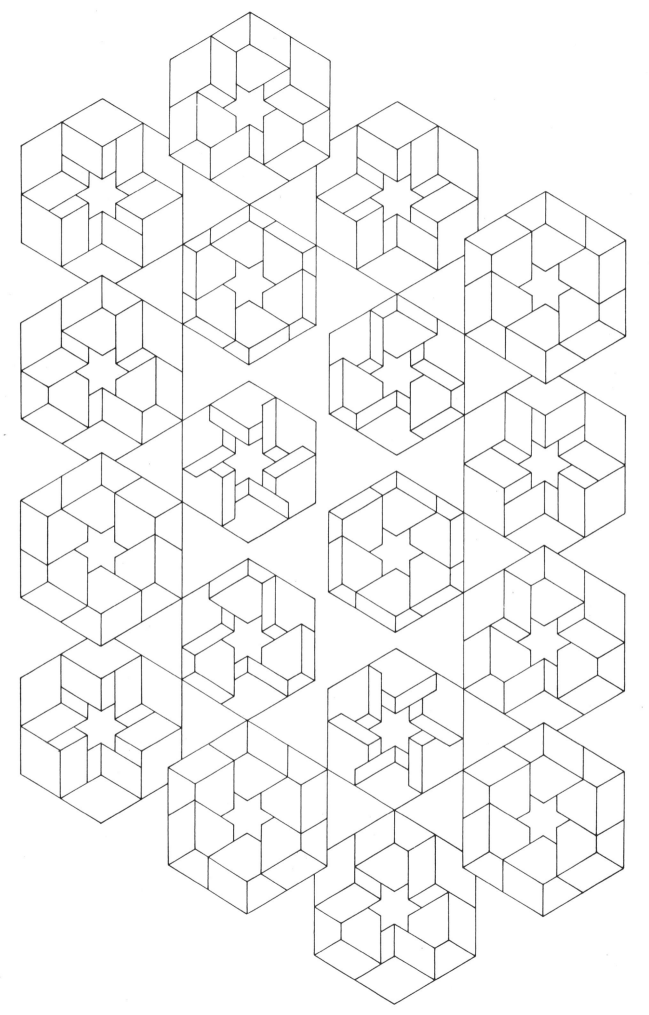

4

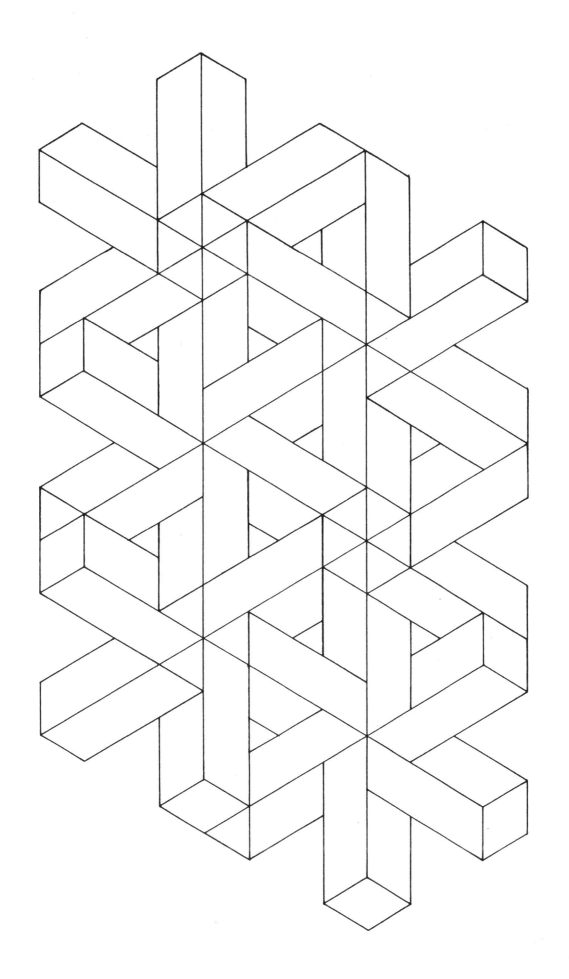

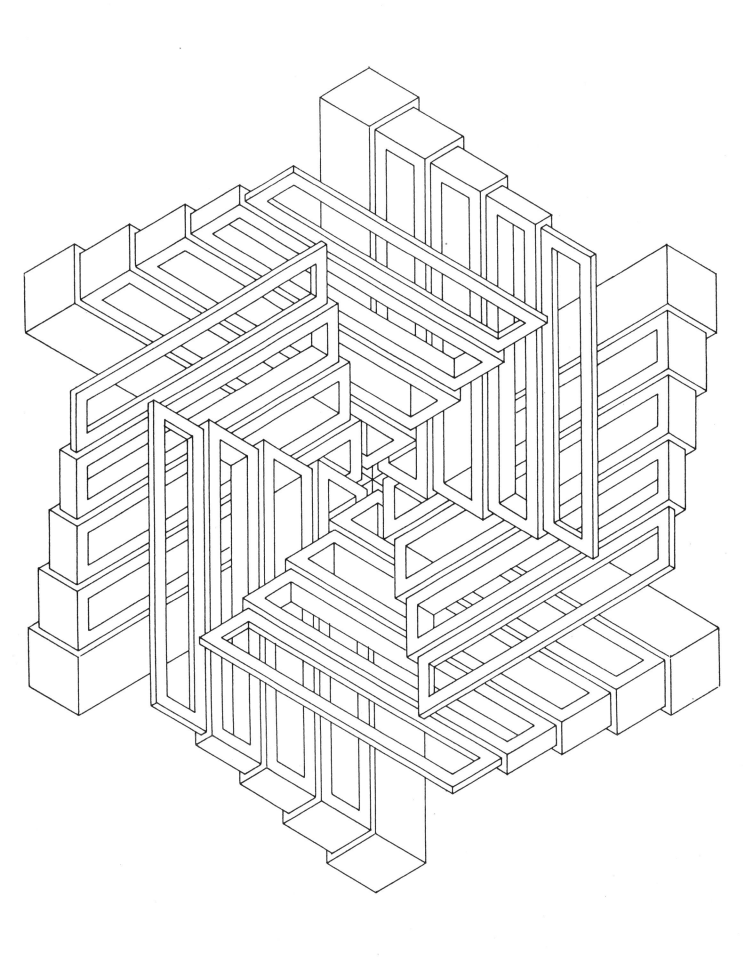

6

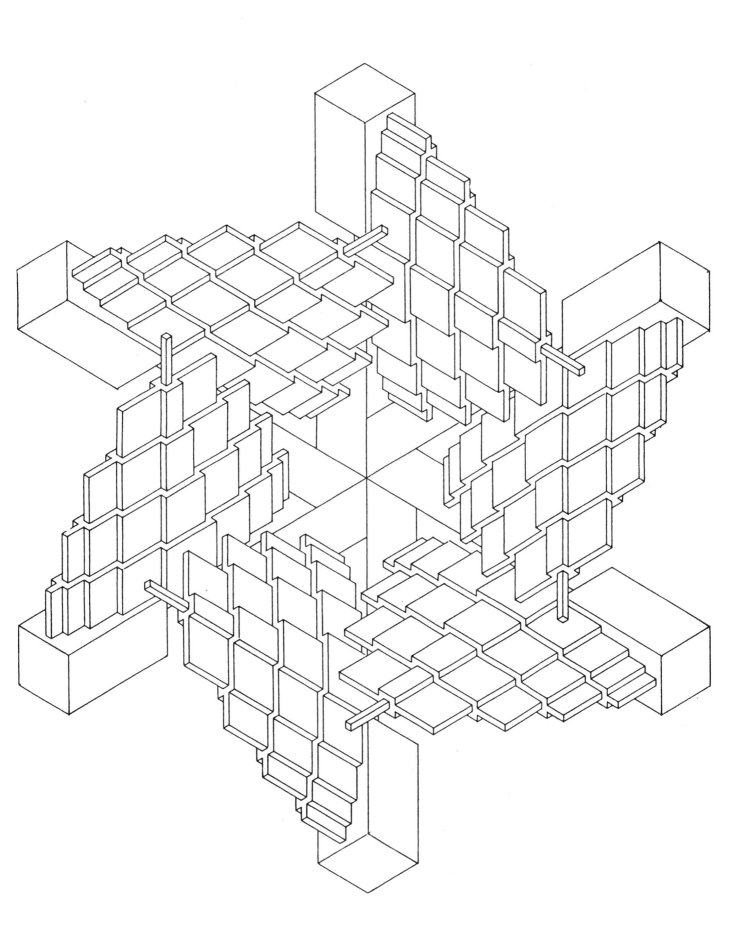

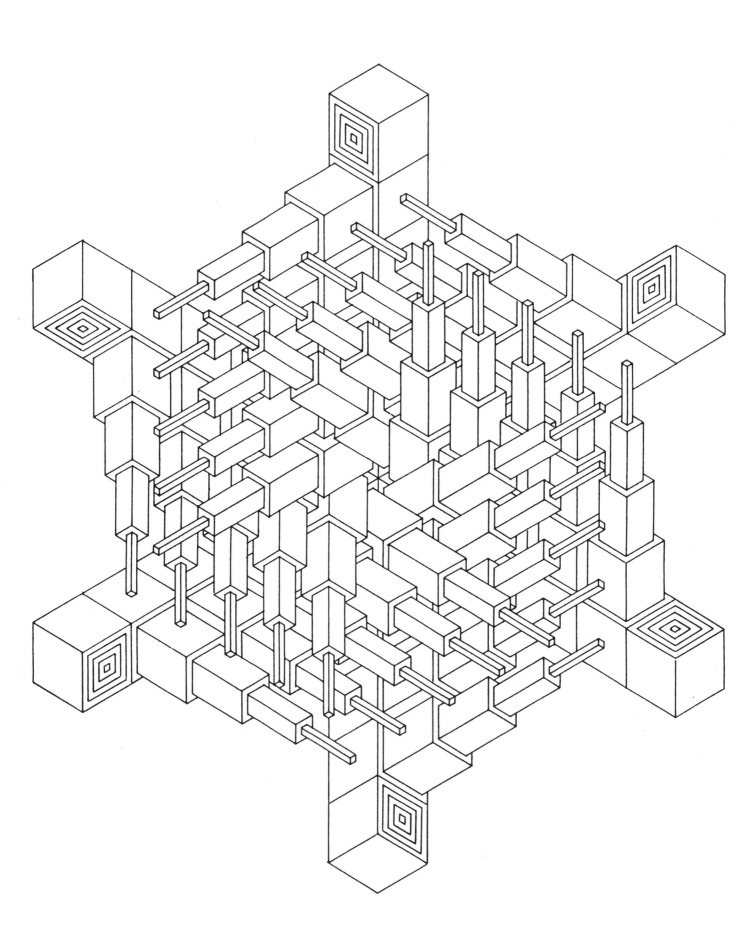

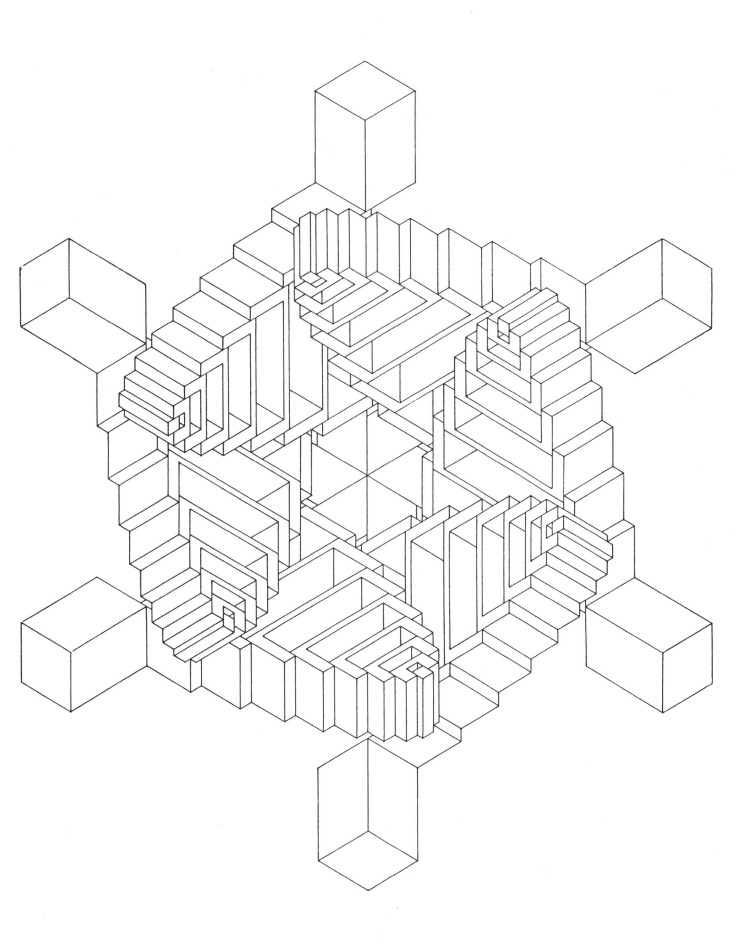

11

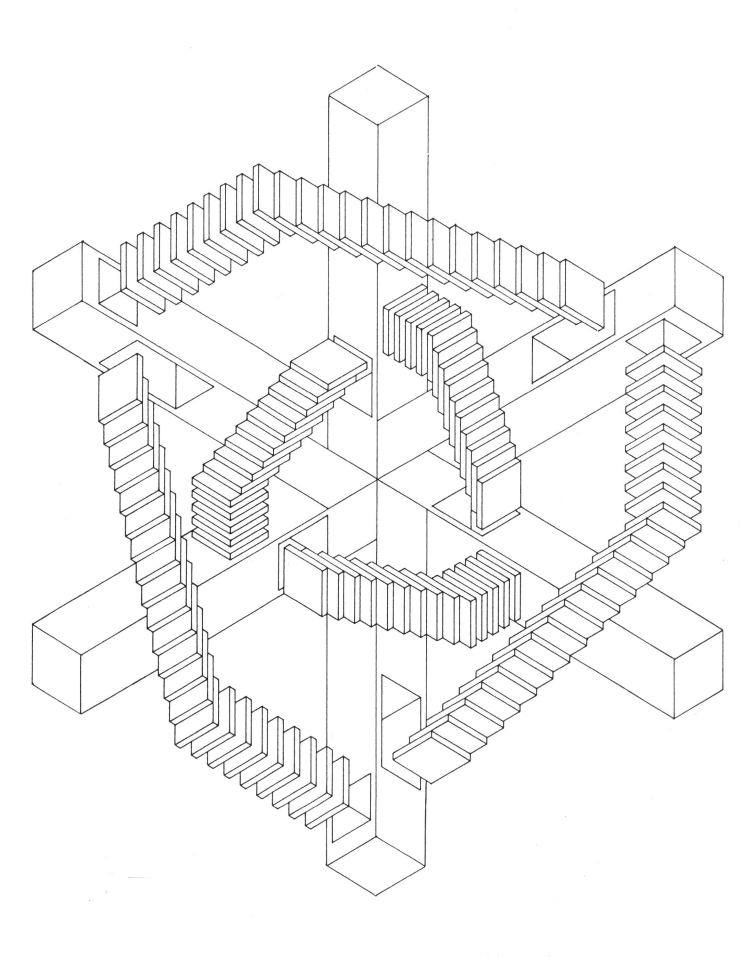

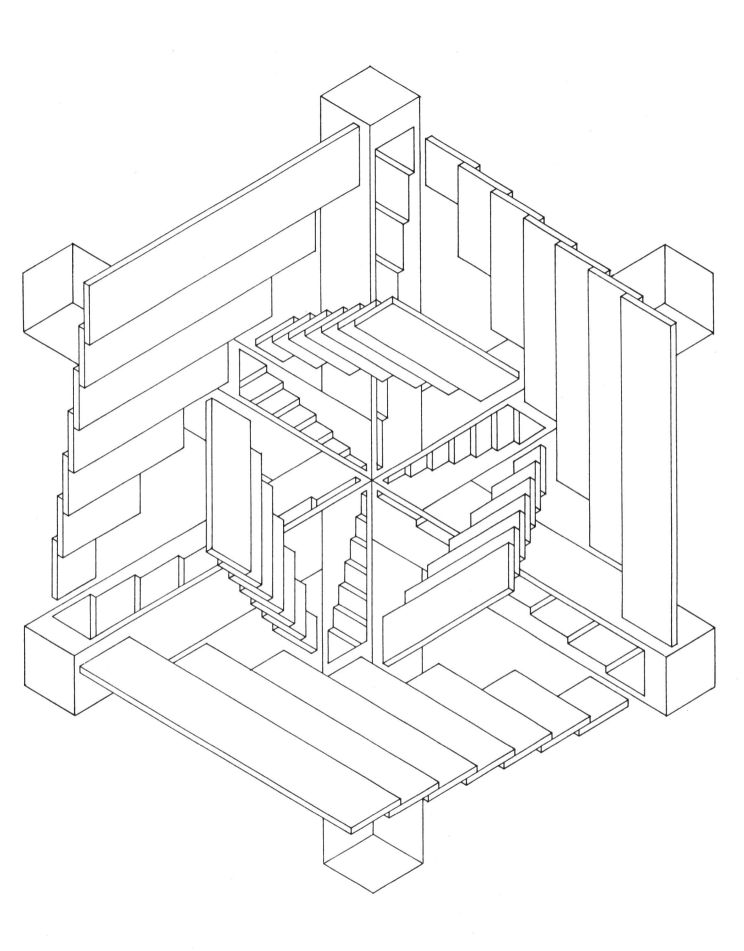

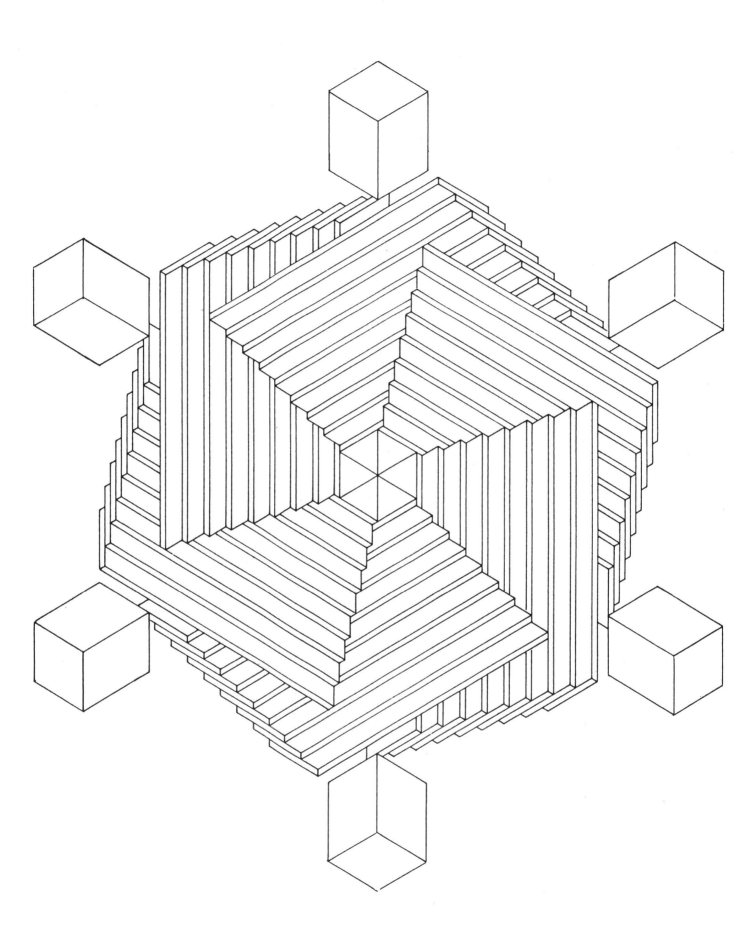

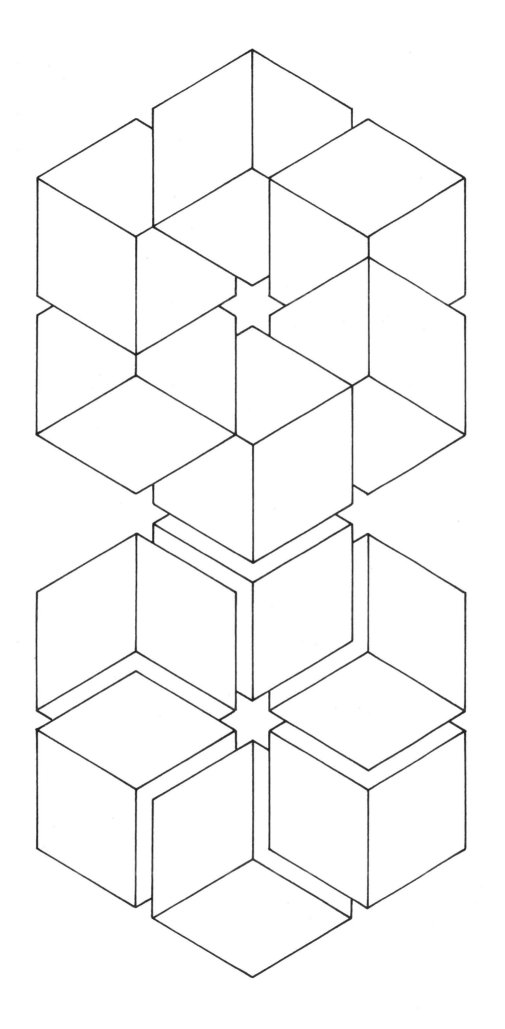

24